Kim D. Ellis

Application of Learning Structures Through Classroom Strategies

aha!

Process, Inc.

Application of
Learning Structures
Through Classroom Strategies

The mission of **aha!** Process, Inc. is to positively impact the education and
lives of individuals in poverty around the world.

Ellis, Kim D.
    Application of Learning Structures Through Classroom Strategies
Kim D. Ellis © 2001. 79 pp.
     ISBN 1-929229-01-1

1. Education 2. Sociology   3. Title

Application of Learning Structures Through Classroom Strategies

CONTENTS

Additional Activities for MODULES 12-16

Module		Page
12	Mental Models	6
13	Planning to Control Impulsivity	27
14	Plan and Label for Academic Tasks	46
15	Question Making	56
16	Sorting Strategies	66

MODULE 12
Mental Models

Objective:
To provide strategies for translating the abstract to the concrete

Mental models can be
2-D visual representations,
a story, or metaphor.

When mental models are directly taught for each discipline, abstract information can be learned much more quickly because the mind has a way to contain or hold the information.

MODULE 12

Mental Models

Page

8   Time perception

9   Time perception: chart

10   Organization of space: arrow activity

11   Organization of space: arrow activity

12   Organization of space: direction activity

13   Organization of space: student difficulties

14   Whole to part

15   Whole to part: example

16   Part to whole

17   Part to whole: example

18   Part to whole: multiple shapes

19   Formal register: mental model

20   Formal register: written expression

21   Formal register: example

22   Mental model: gallon guy

23   Mental model: rounding

24   Mental model: long division

25   Mental model: multiplication of + and - numbers

26   Cognitive strategies

Time

How do you see time?

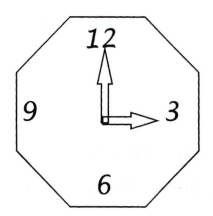

Morning	Noon	Night

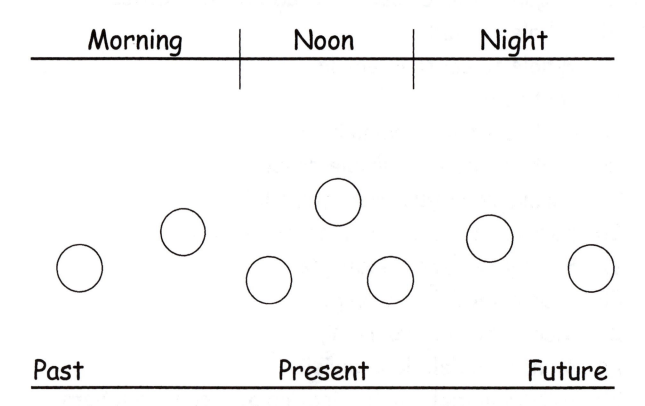

Past   Present   Future

Time

How do you see time?

8:00

8:30

9:00

9:30

10:00

10:30

11:00

11:30

12:00   Lunch

12:30

1:00

1:30

2:00

2:30

3:00

8:00 9:00 10:00 11:00 12:00 1:00 2:00 3:00

Draw a large dot on the side of the point of the arrow that is indicated by left, right, front, or behind in each box. Do not turn your paper as you work.

↑ RIGHT	→ LEFT	↓ FRONT	→ BEHIND	↑ RIGHT
← FRONT	↓ RIGHT	↑ BEHIND	← LEFT	→ FRONT
↓ BEHIND	← RIGHT	↓ LEFT	↑ FRONT	↓ RIGHT
→ LEFT	↑ BEHIND	→ RIGHT	↓ FRONT	↑ RIGHT
↑ BEHIND	↓ FRONT	↑ LEFT	← RIGHT	→ LEFT

Look carefully at each box. If a direction is given, draw a large dot on the side indicated.
If a dot is shown, write the direction in relation to the tip of the arrow. Do not turn your
paper as you work.

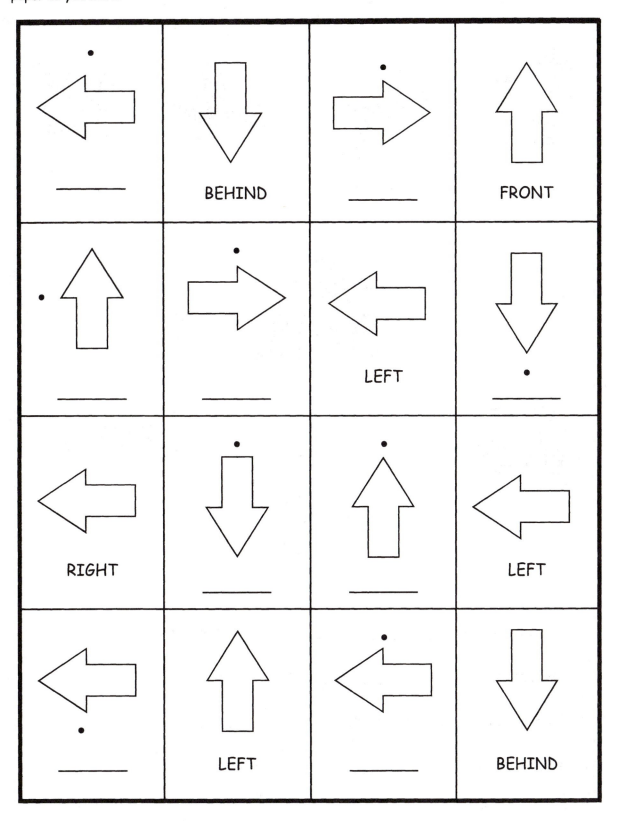

Organization of Space

Position 1

Position 2

Position 3

Position 4

1. The street sign is _____ the person.

2. The car is _____ the person.

3. To the left of the person is the _____ .

4. The house is _____ the person.

Organization of Space

Students could have difficulty in the following areas if they cannot orient space and understand abstract time.

READING
Before, prefixes
After, suffixes
"In the beginning ..."
Sequencing
Author's point of view

WRITING
Descriptive space-order words: first, next, then, etc.
Sequence of steps of a task
Point of view
Writing in third person
Proper placement of punctuation marks

MATH
Place value
Greater than and less than
Definition of field
"Joe is taller than Fred but shorter than Bill"
Probability and outcomes

Whole to Part

Divide each shape into six sections.
Color each section a different color.

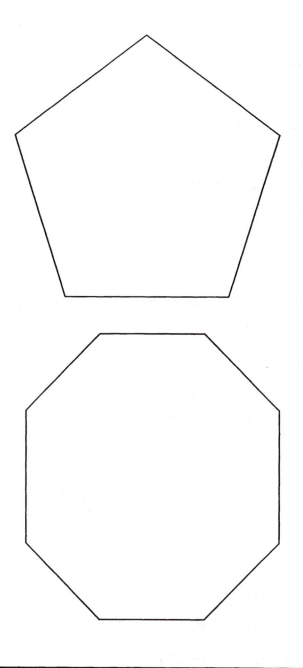

Whole to Part

Divide each shape into six sections.
Color each section a different color.

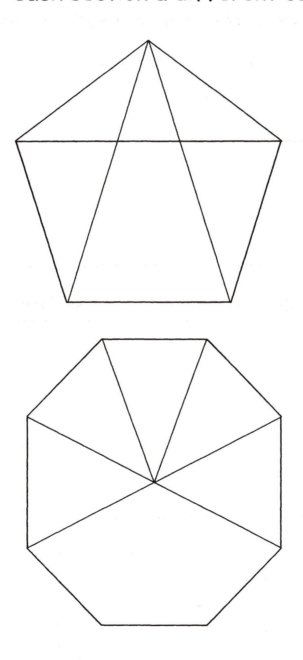

Part to Whole

Using three shapes, create a new image in the box below. Repeat the image in the second box.

After the new image is created, number each section a different number.

After the new image is created, color each section a different color.

Part to Whole

Using three shapes, create a new image in the box below. Repeat the image in the second box.

After the new image is created, color each section a different color.

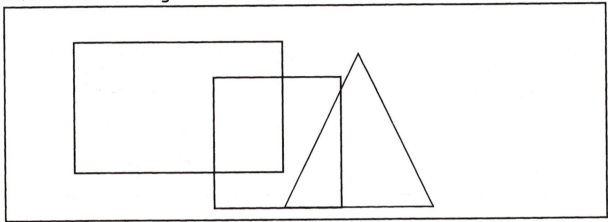

After the new image is created, number each section a different number.

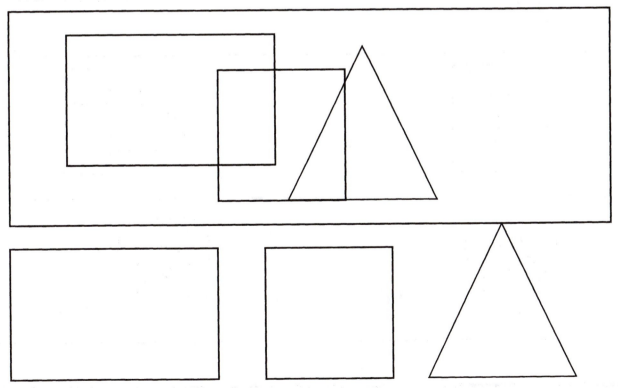

In the figures below, different shapes are used to create a new picture.

Color each section a different color.   Place a number in each section.

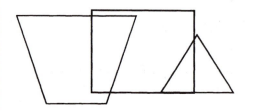
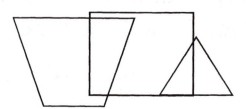

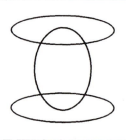
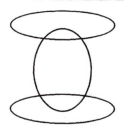

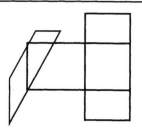
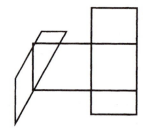

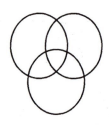
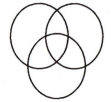

A Mental Model
for
Formal Register

Capital
Letter

Adjectives

Subject
(Noun)

Predicate
(Verb)

Expanders

.!?

Where

How

When

Why

Formal

Casual

Written Expression

Sentence Frame   /‾‾‾‾‾‾‾‾‾‾‾‾‾‾‾. ? !
Reminds me that each sentence must contain a capital letter and some kind of punctuation mark.

Bare-Bones Sentence   /‾‾‾‾‾‾‾‾‾‾‾‾‾. ? !
A sentence must contain a subject and an action.

The subject names a **person**, **place**, **thing**, or **idea**.

The action of the subject expresses **physical** or **mental action**:
      moved   kicked   thought   imagined

Predicate Expanders

The predicate can be expanded by expressing the

△ how   △ when   △ where   △ why   of the action.

Example: The <u>waves</u> pounded relentlessly [how] against the small sailboat [where] because of the violent winds [why] during the storm [when].

Where =	prepositional phrases	to, from, against, behind
How =	adverbs	-ly ending, like or as, with/without
When =	time	before, during, after, when, while, since
Why =	reason	because, to, so, for

(The opening sentence of each new paragraph should contain four expanders.)

Subject describers: Words that describe physical characteristics, personality, numbers, and ownership are describers.

David's Father: Predicate Expander

WHERE

Objective: To teach prepositional phrases as the expander *where*.

Materials: *David's Father* by Robert Munsch

Application:

1. Read *David's Father* to students.

2. Help students build sentences with the expander *where*
    that relate to the story.
    Examples:
    Julie skipped.
    Julie skipped all the way home.
    They went into the kitchen.
    They stood in the middle of the sidewalk.
    They walked down the street.
    The cars jumped into the air.
    Father stomped down the sidewalk.

3. In worksheet form, students will complete the sentences, adding a
    where expander.
    1. Julie was skipping _____.
    2. She ran _____.
    3. Julie looked _____.
    4. Julie jumped _____.
    5. They went _____.
    6. They walked _____.
    7. The cars jumped _____.
    8. The big kids jumped _____.

4. Discuss the mobility of the expander *where*.
    Example: All the way home, Julie skipped.

Gallon Guy

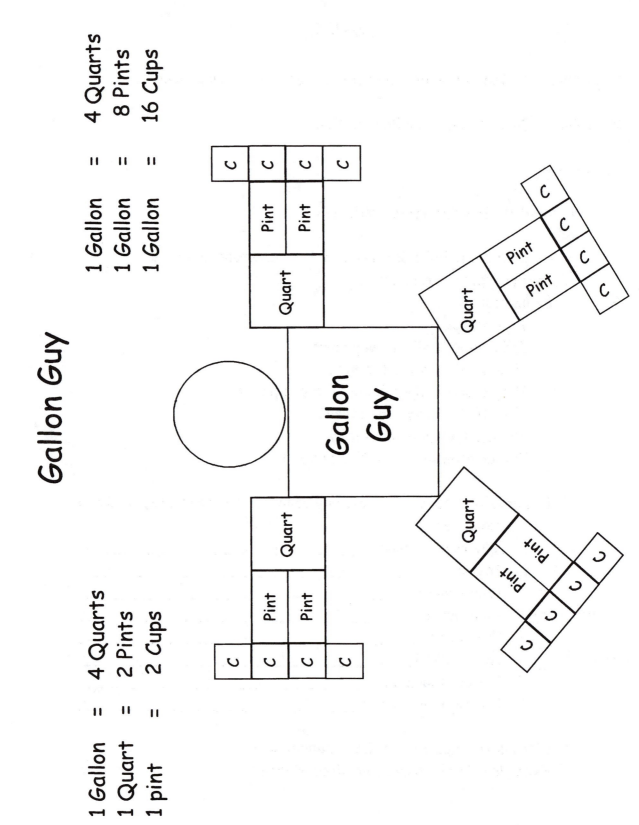

1 Gallon = 4 Quarts
1 Gallon = 8 Pints
1 Gallon = 16 Cups

1 Gallon = 4 Quarts
1 Quart = 2 Pints
1 pint = 2 Cups

Mental Model for Rounding

The rounding roller coaster is an easy way to teach the rounding of numbers. In rounding the 783 to the nearest tens, we underline the 8 and circle the 3. The circled number is the one we locate on the roller coaster.

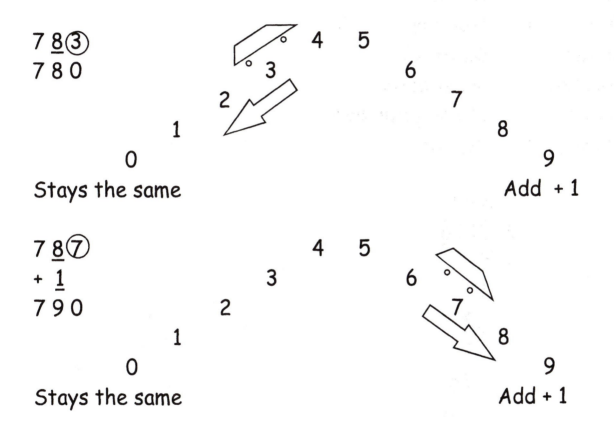

7 8 ③
7 8 0

Stays the same

2   3   4   5
  1   6
0   7
                        8
                          9

Add + 1

7 8 ⑦
+ 1
7 9 0

Stays the same

2   3   4   5
  1   6
0   7
                        8
                          9

Add + 1

Mental Models, cont'd

Long division:

Dad	=	Divide
Mom	=	Multiply
Sister	=	Subtract
Brother	=	Bring down
Cousin	=	Check your work
Rover	=	Repeat

```
         3688
      2 |7376
       -  6
          13
         -12
           17
         - 16
            16
           -16
             0
```

Math Multiplication
+ and - numbers

In the first part of the equation:	In the second half of the equation:
+ numbers are good guys	+ numbers are coming to town
- numbers are bad guys	- numbers are leaving town

+ good guys	X	+ coming to town	= =	+ positive good
+ good guys	X	- leaving town	= =	- negative bad
- bad guys	X	+ coming to town	= =	- negative bad
- bad guys	X	- leaving town	= =	+ positive good

Cognitive Strategies*

INPUT:
quantity and
quality of
data gathered

1. Use planning behaviors.
2. Focus perception on specific stimulus.
3. Control impulsivity.
4. Explore data systematically.
5. Use appropriate and accurate labels.
6. Organize space using stable systems of reference.
7. Orient data in time.
8. Identify constancies across variations.
9. Gather precise and accurate data.
10. Consider two sources of information at once.
11. Organize data (parts of a whole).
12. Visually transport data.

1. Identify and define the problem.
2. Select relevant cues.
3. Compare data.
4. Select appropriate categories of time.
5. Summarize data.
6. Project relationships of data.
7. Use logical data.
8. Test hypothesis.
9. Build inferences.
10. Make a plan using the data.
11. Use appropriate labels.
12. Use data systematically.

ELABORATION:
efficient use
of data

OUTPUT:
communication
of input and
elaboration

1. Communicate clearly the labels and process.
2. Visually transport data correctly.
3. Use precise and accurate language.
4. Control impulsive behavior.

* adapted from the work of Reuven Feuerstein

MODULE 13
Planning to Control Impulsivity

Objective:
To teach students how to develop a plan

If an individual depends upon a random, episodic story structure for memory patterns, lives in an unpredictable environment, and has not developed the ability to plan, then ...

- If an individual cannot plan, he/she cannot predict.
- If an individual cannot predict, he/she cannot identify cause and effect.
- If an individual cannot identify cause and effect, he/she cannot identify consequence.
- If an individual cannot identify consequence, he/she cannot control impulsivity.
- If an individual cannot control impulsivity, he/she has an inclination toward criminal behavior.

MODULE 13

Planning to Control Impulsivity

Page

29 Visual transfer: activity

30 Visual transfer: activity

31 Following specific directions

32 Plan and label: dots activity

33 Plan and label: student-created dots activity

34 Plan and label: student-created dots activity

35 Plan and label: student-created dots activity

36 Plan and label: graph for picture transfer

37 Plan and label: graph for picture transfer

38 Plan and label: graph for picture transfer

39 Plan and label: combination of sets

40 Plan and label: combination of sets

41 Plan and label: combination of sets

42 Plan and label: step sheet

43 Mental model: classificatory writing

44 Planning: research calendar

45 Planning: reading contract

Look at the design on the left. Copy the design in the next frame.

Look at the design on the left. Copy the design in the next frame.

Look at the sample. In each of the two frames, make a new drawing using **only** the changes indicated.

	number color size form	number color size form
	number color size form	number color size form
	number color size form	number color size form
	number color size form	number color size form
	number color size form	number color size form
	number color size form	number color size form

Look at the model on the left. Decide which dots can be connected to match the model. The new shapes must be the exact size and shape as the model. All of the dots must be used.

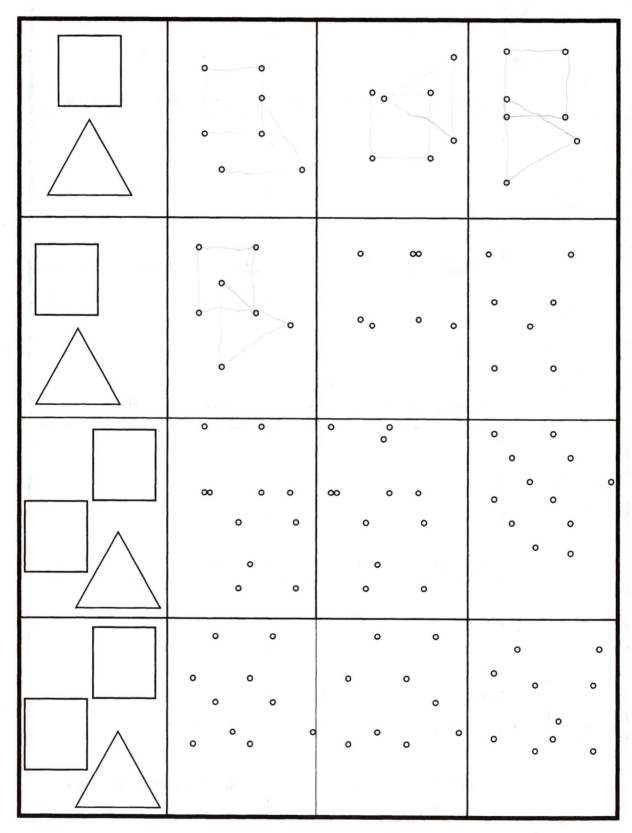

Cut out the three shapes at the bottom of the page. Using the shapes, create your own dot-transfer page.

Cut out the three shapes at the bottom of the page. Using the shapes, create your own dot-transfer page.

Cut out the three shapes at the bottom of the page. Using the shapes, create your own dot-transfer page.

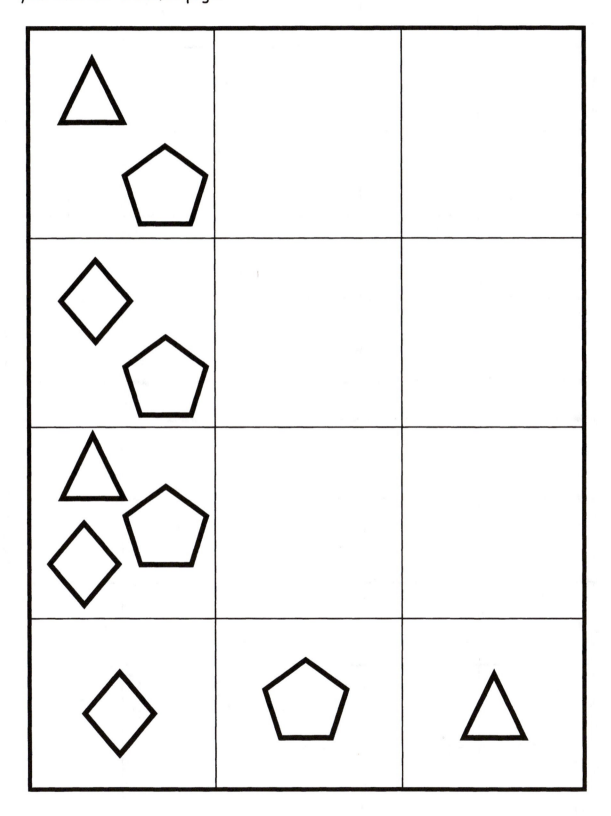

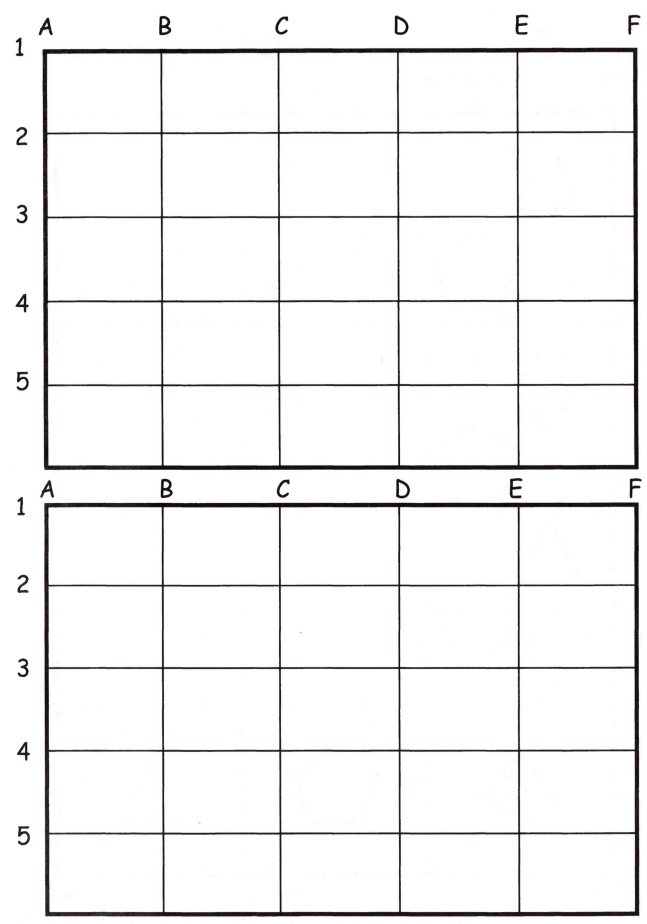

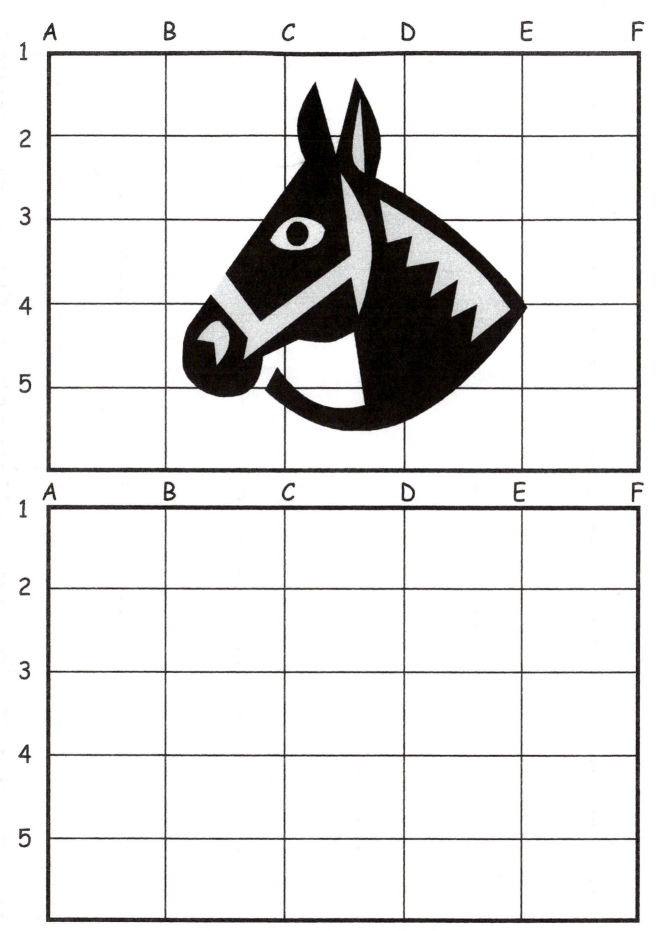

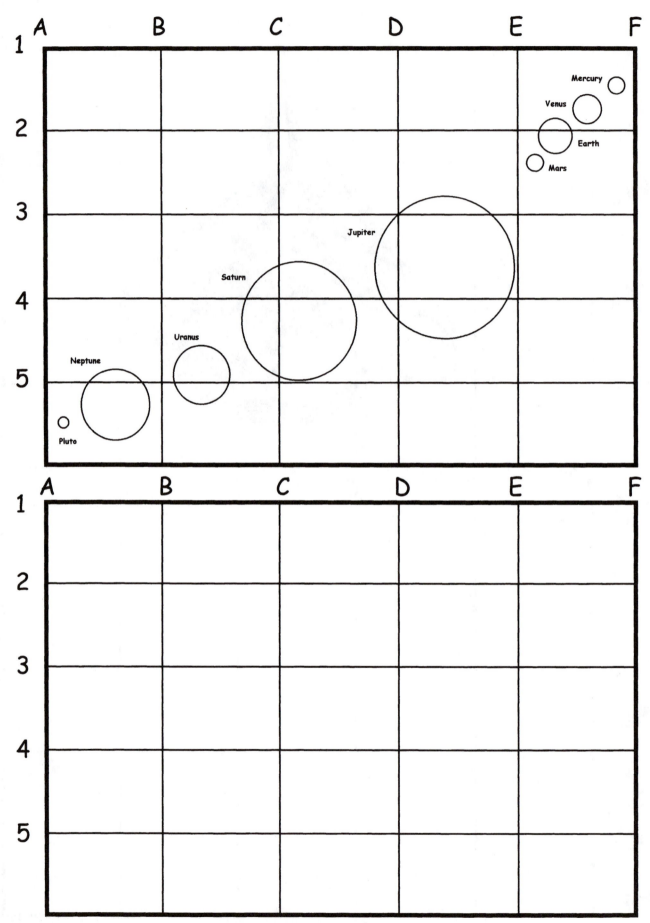

NAME _____

Take a figure from Column 1 and combine it with
a figure from Column 2 to make the shape to the
right of this information. Put the number and
letter that create the original shape on
the line in the middle.

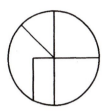

Column 1   ## Column 2

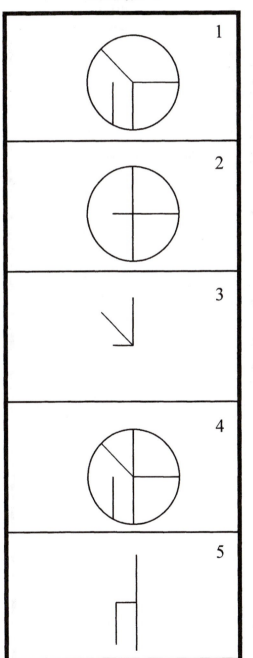 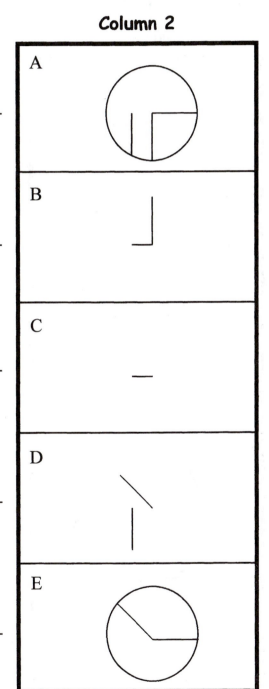

NAME _____

Take a figure from Column 1 and combine it
with a figure from Column 2 to make the
shape to the right of this information. Put
the number and letter that create the original
shape on the line in the middle.

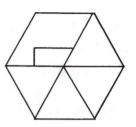

Column 1

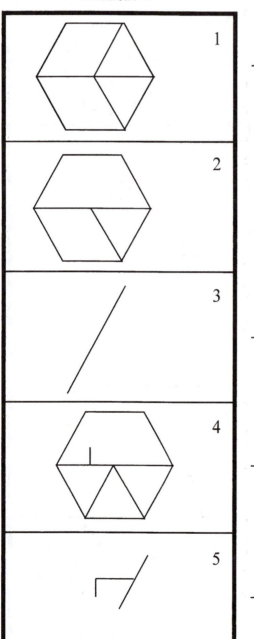

Column 2

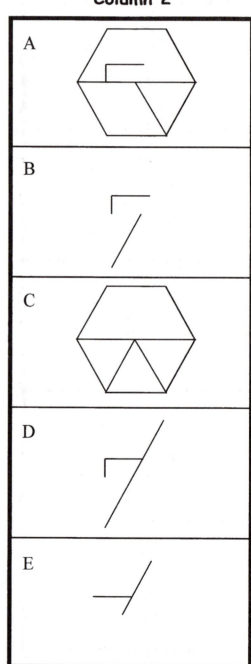

© **aha!** Process, Inc. • (800) 424-9484

NAME _____

Take a figure from Column 1 and combine it
with a figure from Column 2 to make the
shape to the right of this information.
Put the number and letter that create the
original shape on the line in the middle.

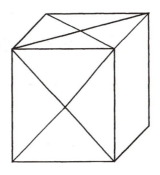

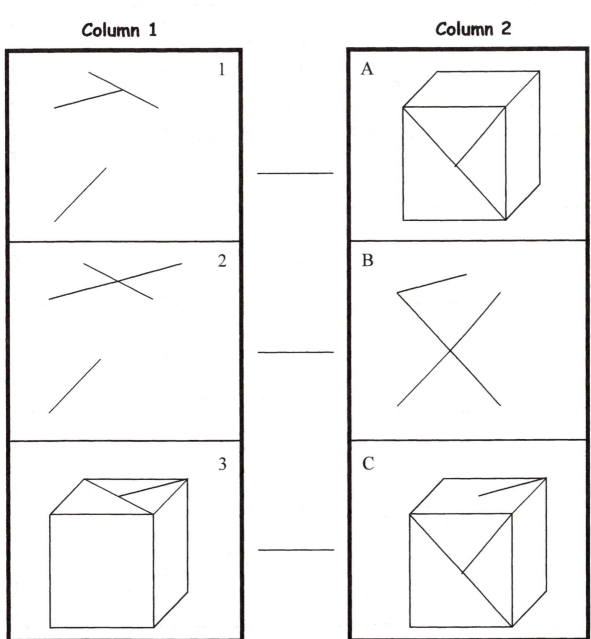

Step Sheet

Plan for today	Goal time	Actual time
1.		
2.		
3.		
4.		
5.		
6.		
7.		

Mental Model for Classificatory Writing

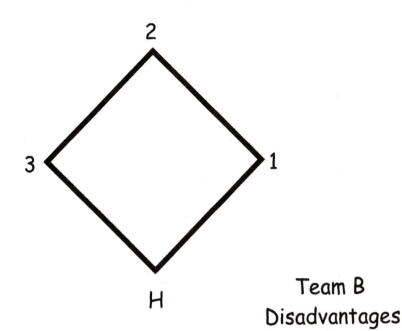

Team A
Advantages

Team B
Disadvantages

1. Opening sentence (H)
   Supporting sentence (1)
   Supporting sentence (2)
   Supporting sentence (3)
   Closing sentence (H)

2. Opening sentence
   Supporting sentence
   Supporting sentence
   Supporting sentence
   Closing sentence

3. Opening sentence
   Supporting sentence
   Supporting sentence
   Supporting sentence
   Closing sentence

1. Opening sentence (H)
   Supporting sentence (1)
   Supporting sentence (2)
   Supporting sentence (3)
   Closing sentence (H)

2. Opening sentence
   Supporting sentence
   Supporting sentence
   Supporting sentence
   Closing sentence

3. Opening sentence
   Supporting sentence
   Supporting sentence
   Supporting sentence
   Closing sentence

Research Calendar

March 1 Library	March 2 Library	March 3 Library	March 4 Library	March 5 Library
March 8	March 9	March 10 10 source cards due	March 11	March 12
March 15	March 16	March 17 Outline due	March 18	March 19
March 22	March 23	March 24	March 25	March 26
March 29	March 30	March 31 50 note cards due	April 1	April 2 Holiday
April 5 Holiday	April 6	April 7	April 8 Rough draft due	April 9
April 12	April 13	April 14	April 15	April 16
April 19	April 20	April 21	April 22 Final draft due	April 23 Oral presentation

Reading Contract

Setting goals will help me to be successful in all areas of life. To become a good reader, I must read daily.

My goal is to read _____ minutes each day. I will read carefully so that I can maintain an average of _____ on my independent reading tests and accumulate a total of _____ points by the end of each grading period.

	GOAL		ACTUAL	
	Grade	Points	Grade	Points
1st gr. period	_____	_____	_____	_____
2nd gr. period	_____	_____	_____	_____
3rd gr. period	_____	_____	_____	_____
4th gr. period	_____	_____	_____	_____

_____   _____
Student's name   Student's signature

_____   _____
Parent's signature   Teacher's signature

MODULE 14
Plan and Label
for
Academic Tasks

Objective:
*To teach procedural plans for the
content areas*

For a task to be done correctly,
a student must have a plan, procedure,
and labels (vocabulary).
Labels are the "tools" the mind uses
to address the task.
Four ways to systematically label are:
numbering, lettering, assigning
symbols, and color-coding.

MODULE 14

Plan and Label
for
Academic Tasks

Page

48 Plan and label: reading strategies
49 Plan and label: story
50 Plan and label: story graphic organizer
51 Plan and label: story map
52 Plan and label: story plot chart
53 Plan and label: narrative rubric
54 Plan and label: classificatory rubric
55 Plan and label: math

Reading Strategies

1. Box in and read the title.
2. Trace and number the paragraphs.
3. Stop and think at the end of each paragraph to identify a key point.
4. Circle the key word or write the key point in the margin.
5. Read the questions.
6. Prove your answer. Locate the paragraph where the answer is found.
7. Mark or write your answer.

1.

2.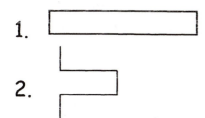

3. S T

4. ⬭

5. ⬭ ⬭

6. P #

7. ⬮

Baker Boy

When my father was a boy in northern Michigan, the annual Cherry Festival was an exciting event. The cherry pie baking contest always drew a large number of entries, including many from children. This allowed these beginning chefs a chance to practice for the future. The grand prize was a 6-inch-wide sweepstakes ribbon and the winner's picture featured on the front page of the county newspaper.

When my father was 11, he decided to enter the contest. No boy had ever won. In fact, no boy had ever entered! He was convinced he had the necessary cooking skills since he made his own breakfast every morning and had learned cooking measurements in school. Baking an award-winning pie didn't sound difficult to him at all.

For weeks he saved his money to buy the things that would be needed. He read recipe books and talked to friends of his grandmother to find out their secrets. Mrs. Johannsen told him how he must handle the crust like a delicate china dish. Mrs. Bowen confided that her secret ingredient was almond flavoring in the filling to give it a special taste. He thought about all these tips as he planned his project.

By the day before the contest, he had practiced rolling out piecrust eight times. He never doubted that he could win.

The day of the contest, he got up before the sun rose. All morning he mixed flour, sugar, shortening, spices, cherries, creamery butter from their farm, and the secret weapon, almond flavoring. He made two pies, in order to have double the chance of getting a perfect one for the contest.

The pies baked in the oven for 45 minutes. Finally the timer rang, and he opened the door. There were two of the most perfect golden-crusted pies that he had ever seen.

When my father presented his best pie to the committee, there was quite a stir. After lunch the judges closed the doors to the hall and began their deliberation. They had to taste each pie and judge it on its flaky crust, tasty filling, and mouth-watering spices. Two hour later they announced their decision. No. 5 had won! Imagine everyone's surprise when the judges presented the blue ribbon to an 11-year-old boy!

Texas Assessment of Academic Skills, 1996

Title:

Author:

Setting:	Three main characters:	Conflict or problem:
Time Place		
Events: Beginning	Middle	End

Story Map

Draw and label three characters in the book:

Show the setting:

Write the problem in the story:

Draw the solution:

Story Plot Chart

Title:

Author:

Setting:

    Time:

    Place:

    General:

    Specific:

Problem or goal:

Circle one:

MAN against MAN   MAN against NATURE   MAN against SELF

Events:

    1.

    2.

    3.

    4.

    5.

Event that solved the problem:

Message of theme:

Narrative Writing

	Yes	Not yet
Setting /When\ & /Where\		
Characters described		
Problem/conflict		
Events 1, 2, 3, 4, 5		
Solution/conclusion		
Strong, vivid language Subject describers		
Fluency (_____ words)		
Legibility		

Classificatory Writing

	Yes	Not yet
Opening (restate prompt)		
Three good things/advantages (two sentences per idea)		
Three bad things/disadvantages (two sentences per idea)		
⟪Why⟫ **Six "why" statements**		
Conclusion (restate prompt)		
Vivid language (10 examples) — subject describers / adjectives		
Legibility		
Fluency # of words counted _____ # required _____		

Math

Think ???

What function is needed?

Which words give me clues?

Read the **question** carefully.

Information

Circle the numbers I will need.

Mark out irrelevant text.

Plan

What is my plan?

What model will I use?

How will I show my work?

Solution

Recheck all information before writing answer.

MODULE 15
Question Making

Objective:
To teach students the process of writing and understanding questions

To perform any task, one must be able to go inside the head and ask questions.
If individuals cannot, then they cannot examine any behavior, nor can they retrieve information in a systematic way.

Students must be able to formulate questions syntactically because without this ability the mind literally cannot know what it knows.

MODULE 15

Question Making

Page

58 Question making: rules
59 Question making: using dice
60 Question making: non-fiction passage/answers given
61 Question making: reading-question stems
62 Question making: non-fiction passage
63 Question making: questions given for p. 62
64 Question making: problem solving in math
65 Question making: problem solving with graph

Rules for Question Making

Question:

_____

_____

Answers:

A. _____

B. _____

C. _____

D. _____

Question:

_____

_____

Answers:

A. _____

B. _____

C. _____

D. _____

Rules:

1. Only one right answer.
2. One wrong answer may be funny.
3. May not use "all of the above" or "none of the above."

Question Making

With a partner, roll the die to determine the type of question to write.

1. Who?
2. Where?
3. What?
4. When?
5. How?
6. Your choice.

Question: _____

_____

A. _____
B. _____
C. _____
D. _____

Question: _____

_____

A. _____
B. _____
C. _____
D. _____

Whales

Did you know that some whales do not have teeth? The baleen whales do not have teeth but have hundreds of thin plates in their mouth instead. These plates, called baleen, strain out food from the water. Baleen whales eat plankton—tiny animal and plant life that drifts in the ocean. The blue whale, the largest animal in the world today, is a baleen whale. It may grow to be 100 feet in length.

Many other whales have teeth and are called toothed whales. They eat squid, fish, and other animals. Toothed whales use their teeth to catch their prey, but they swallow their food whole instead of chewing it. The male narwhal is perhaps the strangest-looking of the toothed whales. It has one tooth that grows out of its upper lip, forming a long, twisted tusk.

Write a multiple-choice question, along with three wrong answers for the correct answer below.

1. Q _____
     a. _____
     b. Baleen whales eat tiny plant and animal life called plankton.
     c. _____
     d. _____

2. Q _____
     a. _____
     b. _____
     c. The blue whale may grow as long as 100 feet.
     d. _____

3. Q _____
     a. Toothed whales swallow their food whole instead of chewing.
     b. _____
     c. _____
     d. _____

Write two additional questions on the back of the paper.

Reading-Question Stems

Word meaning:
    In this story the word _____ means . . . . . ?
    The word _____ in this passage means . . . . . ?

Supporting ideas:
    What did _____ do after . . . . . ?
    What happened just before _____ . . . . . ?
    What did _____ do first?
    Where does this story take place?
    When does the story take place?

Summarizing written texts:
    Which sentence tells the main idea of the story?
    This story is mainly about . . . . . ?
    What is the main idea of paragraph ___ ?
    Which statement best summarizes this passage (paragraph)?

Perceiving relationships and recognizing outcomes:
    Why did _____ (name) do _____ (action)?
    What will happen as a result of _____ ?
    Based on the information, which is _____ most likely to do?
    What will happen to _____ in this story?
    You can tell from this passage that _____ is most likely to . . . . . ?

Analyzing information to make inferences and generalizations:
    How did _____ feel about _____ ?
    How does _____ feel at the beginning (end) of the story?
    According to Figure 1, what . . . . . ? (where, when, how many?)
    By _____ (action), _____ (name) was able to show that . . . . . ?
    The _____ (event) is being held in order to . . . . . ?
    You can tell from this passage that . . . . . ?
    Which word best describes _____ feelings in this passage?
    Which of these is a fact expressed in this passage?
    Which of these is an opinion expressed in this passage?

How Do Plants Trap and Eat Insects?

A plant that eats insects? Can it be true? Yes, it can! There are some plants that trap and digest insects in order to live. These carnivorous plants feed on animal life.

All plants need a chemical called nitrate in order to grow. Most can get nitrate right from the ground. But soils in damp places such as swamps do not have much nitrate, so some plants that live in swamps get nitrate by eating insects.

The Venus's-Flytrap

One plant that eats insects is the Venus's-flytrap. On the edges of the leaves are sharp thorns that look like claws. Each leaf has little hairs on it. When the hairs are touched, the leaf folds itself in half. The claws lock together, and the insect cannot get out. A special liquid inside the plant helps digest the insect.

The Sundew Plant

The sundew plant also has leaves that are covered with little hairs. On each of these hairs is a drop of very sticky liquid. When the sun shines on the plant, the liquid sparkles and attracts insects. But any insect that touches the plant is stuck for sure! The plant hairs close slowly. Then the sundew plant's special liquid digests the insect.

The Pitcher Plant

The pitcher plant does not just trap insects, it drowns them! This plant is shaped like a tube and catches rainwater. Insects are attracted to it because of a sweet, honey-like liquid. The liquid is slippery, and the insects have to work hard not to slide in. After a while, they become tired, fall down the tube, and drown.

These strange plants show that there are many ways for plants to get food to live and grow.

Using the insects story, write one correct and three incorrect answers to the following questions.

1. What happens when an insect lands on the leaf of a Venus's-flytrap?
   A. _____
   B. _____
   C. _____
   D. _____

2. The word carnivorous in this passage means _____
   A. _____
   B. _____
   C. _____
   D. _____

3. The plants in this passage feed on insects because the insects _____
   A. _____
   B. _____
   C. _____
   D. _____

4. You are most likely to find the insect-eating plants in _____
   A. _____
   B. _____
   C. _____
   D. _____

5. Which of these is a FACT about insect-eating plants?
   A. _____
   B. _____
   C. _____
   D. _____

Question Making
for Math

Use the following information to create a problem-solving question.

A pet store has two tanks of goldfish and five tanks of tropical fish. There are 15 fish in each tank. The fish eat every morning and night.

Question: _____

_____

A. _____

B. _____

C. _____

D. _____

Use the same information to create a different problem.

Question: _____

_____

A. _____

B. _____

C. _____

D. _____

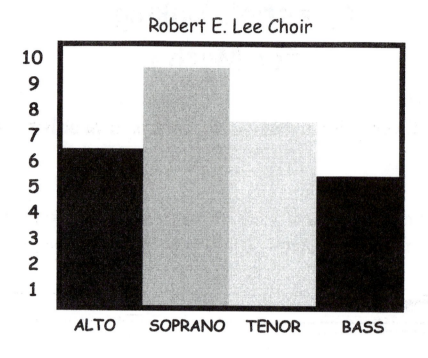

Robert E. Lee Choir

Use the information from the chart to create two problem-solving questions.

Question: _____

_____

A. _____

B. _____

C. _____

D. _____

Question: _____

_____

A. _____

B. _____

C. _____

D. _____

MODULE 16
Sorting Strategies

Objective:

To teach students how to sort concrete and abstract information

To sort and retrieve information, one must be able to sort using criteria and patterns.

Criteria may be:

Structure	Purpose
Number	Size
Direction	Color
Shape	Detail
Type	Pattern
Function	Design

MODULE 16

Sorting Strategies

Page

68 Sorting: patterns with shapes
69 Sorting: characteristics with pictures
70 Sorting: characteristics with pictures
71 Sorting: answer page for pp. 69-70
72 Sorting: information using a test tree
73 Sorting: information for research folder
74 Sorting: information for novel folder
75 Sorting: types of problems for math folder

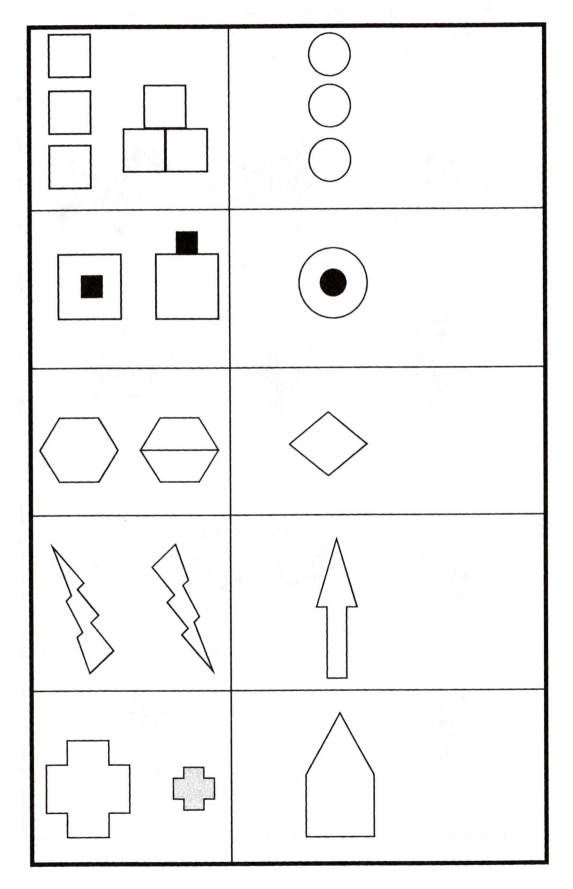

On a separate sheet of paper, list three ways in which the
pictures in each row are alike and three ways they are different.

1.

2.

3.

4.

On a separate sheet of paper, list three ways in which the pictures in each row are alike and three ways they are different.

1.

2.

3.

4.

1   Alike   Different

    1. _____   _____
    2. _____   _____
    3. _____   _____

2   Alike   Different

    1. _____   _____
    2. _____   _____
    3. _____   _____

3   Alike   Different

    1. _____   _____
    2. _____   _____
    3. _____   _____

4   Alike   Different

    1. _____   _____
    2. _____   _____
    3. _____   _____

Test Tree

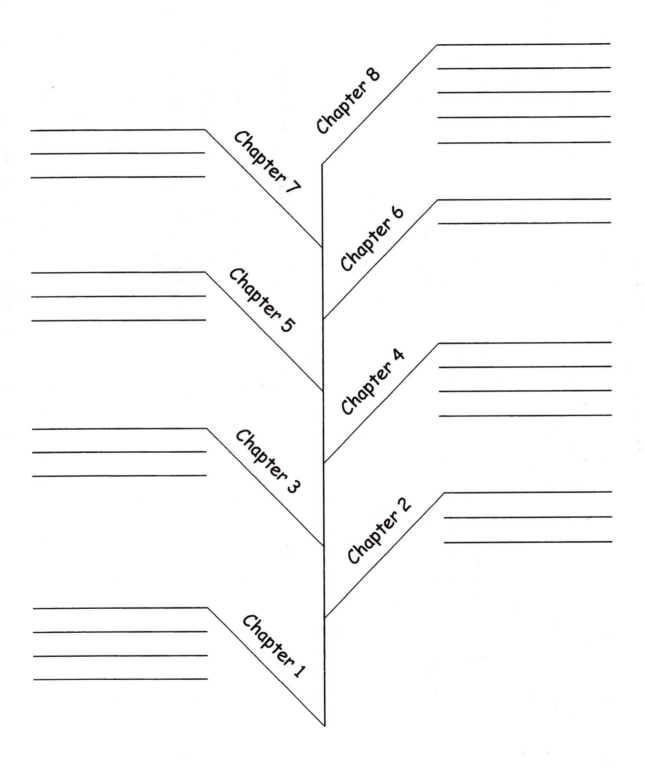

Chapter 8

Chapter 7

Chapter 6

Chapter 5

Chapter 4

Chapter 3

Chapter 2

Chapter 1

Research Folder

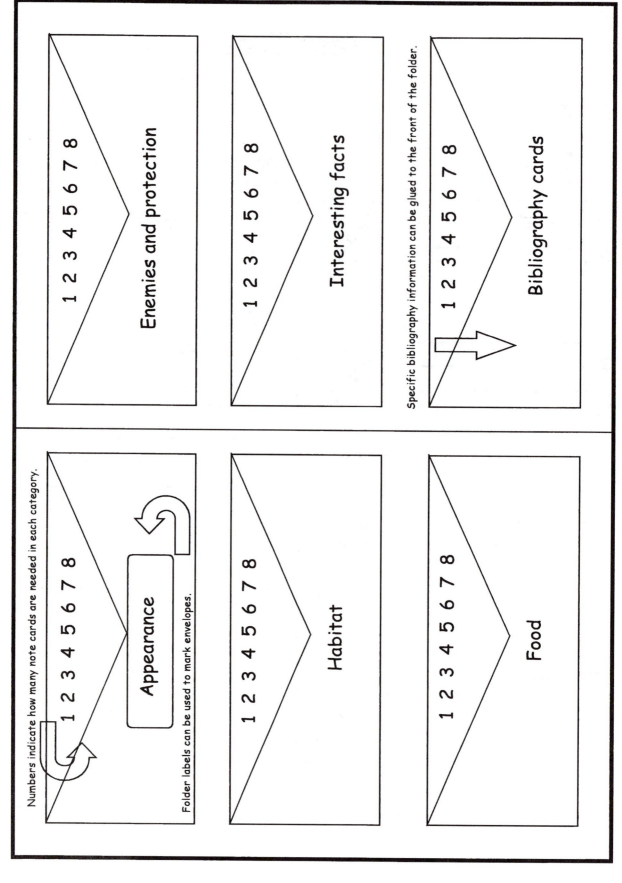

Numbers indicate how many note cards are needed in each category.

1 2 3 4 5 6 7 8

Appearance

Folder labels can be used to mark envelopes.

1 2 3 4 5 6 7 8

Habitat

1 2 3 4 5 6 7 8

Food

1 2 3 4 5 6 7 8

Enemies and protection

1 2 3 4 5 6 7 8

Interesting facts

Specific bibliography information can be glued to the front of the folder.

1 2 3 4 5 6 7 8

Bibliography cards

Novel Folder

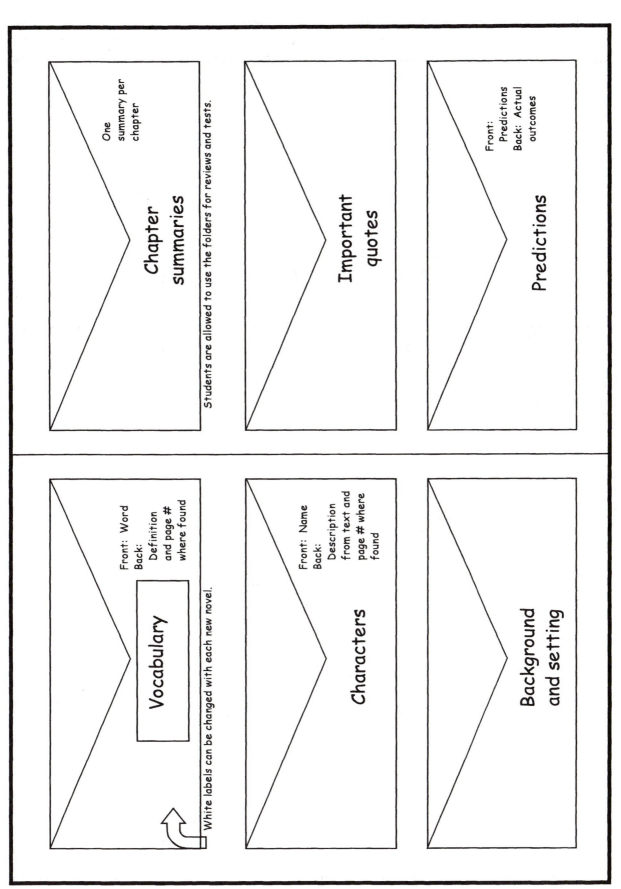

Chapter summaries — One summary per chapter

Important quotes

Predictions — Front: Predictions Back: Actual outcomes

Students are allowed to use the folders for reviews and tests.

Vocabulary — Front: Word Back: Definition and page # where found

White labels can be changed with each new novel.

Characters — Front: Name Back: Description from text and page # where found

Background and setting

Math Folder

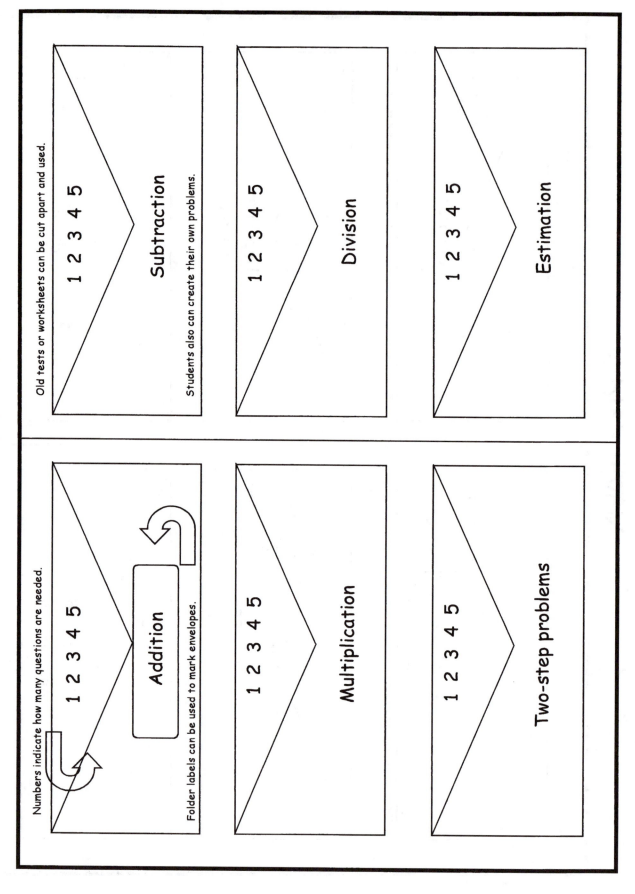

Old tests or worksheets can be cut apart and used.

1 2 3 4 5

Subtraction

Students also can create their own problems.

1 2 3 4 5

Division

1 2 3 4 5

Estimation

Numbers indicate how many questions are needed.

1 2 3 4 5

Addition

Folder labels can be used to mark envelopes.

1 2 3 4 5

Multiplication

1 2 3 4 5

Two-step problems

Activities for Physical Education

Writing:
"How to":   Use a laminated poster board and dry-erase markers to review the steps of games or anything that requires step-by-step instructions.

Intro:
Materials:
Steps:
      1.
      2.
      3.
      4.
      5.
Caution, safety, or warning:
Closing:

Reading:
Sequencing: When you describe or demonstrate a new skill or game, write the steps on sentence strips. In review, scramble the strips and let an "at risk" student put them in order. Sample activities: rhythmic patterns, jump-rope routines, throwing or punting a ball, etc.

Cause and effect: When demonstrating a bounce pass, for example, orally describe, then demonstrate, the proper way. "What would happen if I throw the ball directly at his feet?"

Word meaning: "Guess the Sport." Write terms used in that sport on sentence strips. Place one at a time on the board until the students guess the correct sport.

Math:
Addition/multiplication review: During warm-up, count by 2's, 3's, 4's, etc.
"Mumbo Mumbo":   When a whistle blows, a number is called. Students must assemble themselves in groups of that number. Example: No. 8 is called. Students grab hands to form a group of eight. When the circle is completed, they sit down. On the board, discuss how many groups of eight were made. Were there any left over? If so, why?

"Number Line Relay":   Tape two blank, marked number lines on the floor. Put #'s 1-10 face down in a hula hoop for each team. Run down, pick a number, and put in the correct place on the line.

"Luck of the Draw":   Assemble six decks of cards, cones, and polyspot markers. Divide into teams and run in four heats. Students get a card as they pass the speed bumps. Set music for four minutes. When time is up, count up individual amounts on cards, add team score. Variation: Team

Bibliography

Devine Books, Kids Excel. (1992). *The I Know About Language/Writing Book.* Devine Educational Corporation, P.O. Box 1115, Alvin, TX 77512, (800) 352-EXAM.

Enfield, Mary L., & Greene, Victoria. (1992). *Story Form Comprehensive Guide.* Language Circle Enterprises, P.O. Box 20631, Bloomington, MN 55420, (800) 450-0343, Fax: (612) 884-6787.

Enfield, Mary L., & Greene, Victoria. (1992). *Report Form Comprehensive Guide.* Language Circle Enterprises.

Enfield, Mary L., & Greene, Victoria. (1992). *Written Expression Kit.* Language Circle Enterprises.

Feuerstein, Reuven, & Hoffman, Mildred. (1995). *Organization of Dots.* Palatine, IL: IRI/ Skylight Publishing, Inc.

Feuerstein, Reuven, & Hoffman, Mildred. (1995). *Orientation of Space.* Palatine, IL: IRI/ Skylight Publishing, Inc.

Munsch, Robert. (1983). *David's Father.* Toronto, Canada. Annick Press Ltd.

Payne, Ruby K. (1998). *A Framework for Understanding Poverty.* Highlands, TX: **aha!** Process, Inc.

Sharron, Howard, & Coulter, Martha. (1994). *Changing Children's Minds: Feuerstein's Revolution in the Teaching of Intelligence.* BPC Wheatons Ltd., Exeter, Great Britain.

Skoglund, P., Lucas, M., Lucas, L, & Blaga, J. (1994). *ADD Arithmetic Developed Daily.* Grow Publications, 222 Wolff St., Racine, WI 53402-4268.